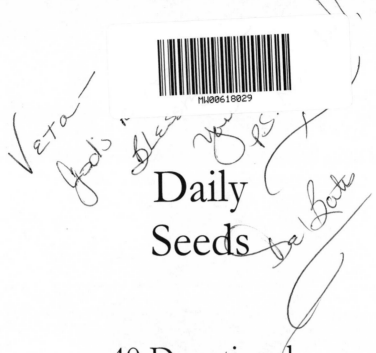

Daily
Seeds

40 Devotional
Seeds of Grace

DEL BATES

Published by EA Books Publishing a division of
Living Parables of Central Florida, Inc. a 501c3
EABooksPublishing.com

ENDORSEMENTS

"Over the years, I've been blessed and privileged to know Jon and Del Bates, finding them to be true followers of our Lord and Savior Jesus Christ.

In *Daily Seeds, 40 Devotional Seeds of Grace*, Del lifts the curtain into her private life with Jesus, offering a warmth and sensitivity that will weave its way into your heart and soul. Unlike some authors, Del writes with a humility that is gentle, quiet, and unassuming, thereby enabling the reader to absorb the depth and spirit of the message without being swamped by the extraneous. This is a book you will want to read ... many times."

Walter Manning
Christian Author/Speaker

"Merriam Webster defines 'seed' as, "the beginning of something which continues to develop or grow." That perfectly describes the deeply personal and poignant reflections on life shared by Del Bates in her book *Daily Seeds*. These seeds of truth based on God's Word will daily encourage your faith and cause you to think you're having a cup of coffee across the table from a good friend."

Pastor Roger Ball
Pastor at Freedom Christian Church
Vero Beach, FL

"I've known Del Bates long enough to trust her heart, her words, and her walk with Jesus. I've also seen the fruit in her life these *Daily Seeds* have borne. You will be enriched on the journey that lies ahead on these pages."

Virelle Kidder
Author of Meet Me at the Well

"For nearly twenty years I've enjoyed reading the work of Del Bates. In critique groups, at workshops and retreats ... the depth of her words, her thinking, her farthest reach to the Father's heart ... have always pulled at my heart strings.

This work is no exception."

Eva Marie Everson
Best-selling author & speaker
President, Word Weavers International

"All readers, regardless of where they are in life's journey, will discover this devotional to be uniquely penned with the guidance of the Holy Spirit. Del Bates, a wife, mother, grandmother, and minister, saturates each page with immense sensitivity, compassion, and depth. You will be captivated with powerful, yet gentle words striking the heartstrings to the tune of supernatural comfort, healing, and strength. With each devotional, Del guides the reader to the Father's voice; supplying nourishment to the soul, while imparting both spiritual and natural insight. Since knowing Del for over 15 years, it is evident, whether sitting still or on bended knee, she is given distinct, clear words to be shared with others. Her gift brings a unique style that embeds her Father's voice in messages to draw hearts closer to God. As portrayed throughout her ministry, Del continues to mirror God in her writings to bring supernatural empowerment. Taking time to explore these truths will be thought provoking and challenging enough to change you for eternity!"

Cheryl M. Hine
Exec. Director, Care Net Pregnancy Center of Indian River County
Senior Minister, Faith United Fellowship

"Del is a woman that has used her life experiences to bring transformation to others. She has a passion for women to embrace the power of the Father's love. I highly recommend this devotional that will warm your heart, and challenge you to receive the promises of God daily."

Joy Green
U.S. Director SE Region, Aglow International

DEDICATION

This book is dedicated to my parents,
Robert and Mary Berdych.
Although you have gone on to be with the Lord
I thank you for all you taught me—

After My Dad passed
I felt his presence one evening.
As if he was there, I could hear him tell me,
"Del, death is only a passing
of one room into the next.
Live it now my daughter
live it, with no regret.

Always speak the truth
never ever lie.
Always tell the truth
and never ever deny.

With those powerful words, my desire to write became all
the more important—
To bring the message of salvation and what I learned in his
passing,

"Eternity Is All That Matters."

CONTENTS

PREFACE

In the beginning—

Daily Seeds began when many only knew that a mouse was something stirring in the house in the tale of The Night Before Christmas. And, your address was where you physically lived, not your residence in cyber-space.

Yes, Daily Seeds began many years ago as a daily devotion on my website when family and friends were excited to get an e-mail in their mailbox.

As the Internet continued to bloom, and advertisements from all around the globe started to blossom, my seeds got weeded out— with that, I took a break from planting them.

Daily we all need encouragement. Life happens—But God! Yes, God is always there. Sometimes we just need a touch of His love and mercy.

So with the encouragement of fellow writers and friends, I've decided to harvest some of the old seeds and mingle them with the new.

My prayer for you is that each day, the Lord will sprout a seed of hope in you. I pray that through daily reflection, that the love of God by the power of the Holy Spirit, and the love of Jesus will enable you to see your life in a whole new way.

And out of His grace and mercy, you will come to a greater understanding of God's unending love for you.

May His Holy Spirit speak to you and encourage you in whatever you are facing each day.

Come along on my journey of Grace, and see what The Lord will do.

1

Are You Prepared

"But about that day or hour no one knows, not even the angels in heaven, nor the Son, but only the Father."
Matthew 24:36

It started out like any other day. Put a batch of clothes in the washer, turn on the dishwasher then heat up the kettle to brew a morning cup of tea. Suddenly silence. Everything stopped, the washing machine, the dishwasher, lights blinked off, "Oh, No!" I cried to my husband, "Overload!"

Since we've had a few scorchers the past few days, I thought our system was experiencing an overload with everyone using abnormal amounts of power. Then, in a flash − for an instant, everything clicked back on.

I raced to charge up every electronic device we had. Our phones, our iPad, the laptop, anything I could think of—I even hurried over to my computer to transfer my writing documents from my desktop to a USB Stick just in case.

Just as my computer confirmed its transfer, the silence returned; this time for good.

We were not prepared. Not one of our gadgets were even one-hundred percent charged. Some were even as low as twenty-percent.

Jesus states in the book of Matthew that no one knows the day nor the hour, not the angels in heaven, nor even the Son of Man, but only the Father knows when He shall return. Will I be ready for that? Will you? The only way we will know for sure is in the way we live our daily lives.

We are to live in the shadow of Jesus and how he lived; caring for the sick, for the homeless and for the least of our brothers. We need to be continually developing our relationship with Him. Daily to be seeking His direction for our lives and listening to the still small voice of His Spirit so that we will be able to walk in the footsteps of Jesus.

Then beloved *if* you are living your life this way, you will be prepared for Jesus' glorious return. Even if the power as we know it in our lives goes out, you will not be in fear, but you will be able to embrace it with a knowing in your heart that this is ultimately what you've waited for all your life; his unexpected, but expectant return.

Prayer for the day: Dear Jesus, help me to be prepared. I know that You told Your disciples, someday You would return to this earth. Help me daily to live my life for You, that I will be ready for the very hour, the very day that it will be.

As you sit down with the Lord today, jot down what you feel He is speaking to your heart.

_____

_____

2

_____

_____

_____

_____

_____

_____

_____

_____

_____

_____

_____

2

Bitter Sweet

"And forgive us our debts, as we also have forgiven our debtors."
Matthew 6:12

Read Proverbs 17:22

Vinegar is a multi-purpose solution. We can easily recognize it by its bitter taste and its strong smell.

One of its most common uses is for salad dressing. Others may use it as a means to shed a few pounds, and someone else to reduce the sting of sunburn; most assuredly I'm sure if you were to Google the word vinegar, there would be thousands of other uses for it.

My husband uses it as a preservative in canning pickles. Since I've only canned sweet things like apples for applesauce, or peaches or pears, this was something new to me. Where my recipe called for a cup or so of sugar, his called for a gallon of vinegar.

Today when I was gathering a few of his half-empty jars

to clean them out, I couldn't believe what I found. As I opened each jar, I discovered that the lids on every jar were pitted, blackened and eaten away.

Yuck! I thought. Because they remained tightly covered for the past year, it allowed the acidity of the vinegar to eat the metal clear away. Wow — the very same acid that was used as a preservative, actually destroyed when it was bottled up.

Beloved, isn't that the same with our thoughts? As we think about things that are good, or even share funny stories with loved ones or friends, and we can suddenly feel a sense of joy spring up, or we might even burst out with a good-old hardy laugh. Proverbs tells us that a merry heart is good for the bones.

On the flip side of that, remember those ugly lids? Pitted was the word. When we choose to harbor ill feelings toward others such as hate or anger or even bitterness, that will have the same effect in our human bodies as the vinegar did to those lids. The writer of Proverbs tells us that envy rots the bones. (Proverb 14:30) Jesus also tells us when the disciples asked Him how to pray, He said, "To forgive us our debts, as we also have forgiven our debtors."

So then, to prevent our lives from ever becoming like those rusty old lids, let us remember the words of Jesus. Let us strive to forgive all who have ever hurt us which will keep us from harboring ill feeling toward others.

Prayer for the day: Dear God. Thank You for forgiving me. I ask You to guide me continually by Your Spirit that whenever I begin to harbor feelings that are not of You, that You will speak to me to forgive immediately so that nothing ill will stay within me.

As you sit down with the Lord today, jot down what you feel He is speaking to your heart.

_____

_____

_____

_____

_____

_____

_____

_____

_____

_____

_____

3

Born Free

"Assuredly, I say to you, whoever does not receive the kingdom of God as a little child will by no means enter it."
Mark 10 :15

I love to take my grandchildren to the park. As soon as we arrived one cool summer day, my little granddaughter, Nina, made a b-line straight to the swings. She raised her little hands right up in the air, "Grandma, please, please help me get up on the swing," she smiled.

I sat on a rock beside her and watched her swing as she tried to reach higher and higher as if to touch the sky. Her little arms pulled her tiny body forward with all her might and her little chest puffed out like a proud dad introducing his newborn baby.

Each time she lifted off the ground, she'd tuck her little feet as close the bottom of the swing as she could. With each pump, she continued to glide higher and higher.

I felt her peace. I felt her freedom. I said to myself, *I*

want that. I want that today, tomorrow and the next day and the next.

Isn't that the way Jesus tells us to come to Him? He says, *Let the little children come to Me, and do not hinder them! For the kingdom of God belongs to such as these. Truly I tell you, whoever does not receive the kingdom of God like a little child will never enter it.*

Those are some pretty harsh words. But as we grow up, we attach ourselves to so many things that are not of God. We become so entangled with the things of this world that we lose our peace. We lose our way and sometimes, as a result, even lose our relationship with God.

Beloved, His desire is for us is to live just like these little children. They know that their parents are there to provide. They look to them for love and security from the time they're born till even up into their teens.

That is simply what God, Our Father, wants us to do. He wants us to let go of our foolish ways, let go of our pride and just come to him as a child in need, humbly knowing that He will provide for every need, every day of our lives.

Nina wanted to get on that swing. She knew what she wanted to do, but that she couldn't make it on her own. God is standing there just the very same way for each of us just like I was there for her.

Prayer for the day: Dear God, Oh the innocence of little children! Help me to take a good look at myself today and see where I am trying to do it on my own and not even asking You for help.

As you sit down with the Lord today, jot down what you feel He is speaking to your heart.

_____

_____

_____

_____

_____

_____

_____

_____

_____

_____

_____

_____

_____

4

Boundless Love

"And he passed in front of Moses, proclaiming, "The LORD, the LORD, the compassionate and gracious God, slow to anger, abounding in love and faithfulness."
Exodus 34:6

God is Love!

Throughout the Old Testament God revealed Himself through many different names. With each name, He was revealing another trait of His character to the children of Israel. Just to name a few, we learned that He is, Jehovah Shalom, a *God of Peace*, Jehovah Jireh, *My Provider*, and Jehovah Nisi, *The Lord is Our Banner.*

If we were to take each one of these names and look up their meanings, each one would be centered around the word 'Love.' In a quote from Abe Burrows, he says, "Love is when another person's needs are as important as your own," but take that exact quote and relate it to God, it would read a little different — "Love is when another person's needs are more important than your own."

He places our needs above His. His desires for us is for us to be *His* people and for *Him* to be our God. His love stems deeper than we can ever imagine and extends wider than we can fathom.

You see, beloved, the love of God has no bounds. With our love, we are always setting up boundaries. *I will do this if he will do that—I will do this if they won't do that.* God is not that way. His love just goes on and on no matter what we do. Even when we disobey Him, yes we break His heart, but He waits for us to realize our wrong, to turn from what we've done and seek His forgiveness.

So if we read about Him as El Shaddai, *The LORD Almighty*, or Adonai, *LORD Master*, or Jehovah Rapha, *The LORD That Heals*, He is still the one true God, the Lord Almighty, who loves each of us beyond anything we can dream or imagine with boundless, unconditional love.

Prayer for the day: Dear Father God, LORD of all, thank You for loving me so much. May I take time today and study Your holy names one by one. My desire is to know more of You that I can love You for all You are to me.

As you sit down with the Lord today, jot down what you feel He is speaking to your heart.

_____

_____

_____

_____

_____

_____

_____

5

Catch Me If You Can

"Those who wait upon the Lord shall renew their strength."
Isaiah 55:8

"Caesar! No! No!" I jumped up from the floor and dashed toward the stairs to grab my little grandson.

Knowing I was not far behind, he glanced back as if to say, "C'mon Grandma, catch me if you can." But, just as he approached the first step, I snatched him up, wisped him in my arms and hurled him upward.

How many times are we just like him? We know that God is moving us on to a new level, and yet we are too impatient to wait. Or, like Caesar, we hear God say, "Wait," then because we've heard part of what He said, we dash ahead regardless of the consequences?

God knows what lies ahead. He knows just how fast we are able to go depending on the circumstances. He also knows that our strength is in Him. And if He does not believe that we are ready for the next step, He'll hold us back to protect us from a fall.

Little Caesar, knew that his playroom was at the top of those stairs. And by his innocent dare, he had no fear in believing he could get there on his own. But as a little child, he wasn't able to comprehend that without my help he couldn't get up to that playroom at all.

You see beloved, the ladder of life is established one step at a time. And with God as our leader, guide, and our protector, He will take us to that new level in our life if we only wait upon him and allow Him to renew our strength each day.

Prayer: Dear Lord, as You give me strength for each day, teach me to wait upon You. Help me to see that haste will only cause waste. I thank You that You are only a word away, and all I need to do is call.

As you sit down with the Lord today, jot down what you feel He is speaking to your heart.

_____

_____

_____

_____

_____

_____

_____

_____

_____

_____

_____

6

Christ In Me

*"And if the Spirit of **him** who raised Jesus from the dead is living **in** you, he who raised Christ from the dead will also give life to your mortal bodies because of his Spirit who lives **in** you."*
Romans 8:11

"Mom," my daughter said, "I know my wedding day was special, but, you need to get beyond the wedding and move on — now it's time for the marriage."

She was right. Three months had passed since their wedding, and I was still printing pictures, making photo albums and creating videos; I was caught up in the fairytale, while she was living in the reality of it.

Sometimes that is what we need to do with Jesus. We know that He died for us, and the precious debt that He paid for each and every one of us. I would never make light of the way that He suffered and died, but we must move on beyond the grave to see the power that we have in Him through His death and resurrection.

21

Our scripture tells us, *And if the Spirit of **him** who raised Jesus from the dead is living **in** you, he who raised Christ from the dead will also give life to your mortal bodies because of his Spirit who lives **in** you.* Paul is telling us that the precious Holy Spirit of God was the dunamis (which is the Greek work for power, comparable to a stick of dynamite) / power which raised Jesus from the dead, and we have that same power in us, to achieve anything that He has called us to do.

If that power was so strong to raise Jesus from the grave, then what does it tell us? There is one song that says it all— Jesus author of Salvation— He rose conquered the grave— forever He will move the mountain, He is mighty to save.

Although it is a song that we usually sing around Eastertime, it says it all. He rose and conquered the grave and that is what we have the ability to do in Him. He wants us to conquer the graves of our lives regarding things that we are stuck in or keeping us from all that He has for us.

So beloved, just as my daughter reminded me to look beyond her wedding and to see the joy of their new life together, Paul also reminds us to look beyond the grave and see the power that we have in the resurrected Christ.

Prayer for the day: Dear Jesus, I know that You died for me. Help me to unleash the power that You have given to me to be able to stand against anything that comes my way today.

As you sit down with the Lord today, jot down what you feel He is speaking to your heart.

_____

_____

_____

_____

_____

_____

_____

_____

_____

_____

_____

_____

_____

7

Ebb Tide

"Then Peter got down out of the boat, walked on the water and came toward Jesus but, when he saw the wind, he was afraid and, beginning to sink, cried out, "Lord, save me!" Immediately Jesus reached out his hand and caught him. "You of little faith," he said, "why did you doubt?"
Matthew 14: 29-31

While I was standing on the boardwalk one Sunday evening, I watched in amazement as a group of surfers rode the breaking waves in the ocean.

Although there were about six or seven teens, I continued to focus on one of the young girls. She rode with grace. She rode with eloquence as the waves carried her in. Even though she took a few crashes, most of her attempts were successful because she only hopped on when she felt it was the perfect wave; not a smaller one that would cause a distraction.

As I watched her climb on that thin little board and then

slowly rock her body to the movement of the water, I was in awe.

In our Christian walk, we are called to do the same; Not to focus on the waves around us, but to focus on Jesus. In our scripture today, it brings us to the story of the disciples where we can see this played out before our eyes. After the miracle of the loaves and the fishes, Jesus sent his disciples to get in the boat and to go to the other side. When they saw the fierce winds begin to blow, they were afraid. Jesus appeared to them and told them not to fear. Then Peter, who was always fleecing Jesus cried out, "Lord, if it is You, tell me to come to You on the water."

"Come," Jesus answered. Peter did get out of the boat and walk to Jesus. As long as he kept His eyes on Jesus, he was ok. But when he focused on the wind, he started to fear, and he cried out, "Lord save me!"

We *must* keep our eyes on Jesus. When we do the same as Peter and take our eyes off Jesus, we too will feel like we are going under. But if we aim to focus on Him, diligently to praying and seeking his face in every single area of our lives, He will be there to extend a hand just as He did to Peter.

Beloved, let us today try to be more like Peter. Like that gal riding her surfboard. Let us keep our eyes off the crashing waves of life and keep our eyes on Jesus.

Prayer for the day: Dear Jesus, help me today to keep my eyes on You. Even though waves may sometimes crash about me, I thank You that Your hand is always outstretched to me.

As you sit down with the Lord today, jot down what you feel He is speaking to your heart.

_____

_____

_____

_____

_____

_____

_____

_____

_____

_____

_____

8

From Glory to Glory

"And all, who with unveiled faces contemplate the Lord's glory, are being transformed into his image with ever-increasing glory, which comes from the Lord, who is the Spirit.
2 Corinthians 3:18

Writing is a craft. Therefore, it takes writing, writing, and re-writing. In the different facets of your work, the toughest part is the final task—having your masterpiece critiqued. Oh, it's easy to write and show it off to family and friends who will praise you for anything that you do, but to take it to a group of seasoned writers, that's a whole different story.

That's where we use the phrase "Read till you bleed." That is where we get out the red pens and cross out this, cross out that and make grammatical suggestions.

We have a particular method in our little groups. It's called the sandwich method. First, we praise, then we find stumbling blocks within, and finally we end with praise for a job well done and encourage our fellow writers.

Our Heavenly Father is the same with us. He doesn't condemn us when we have messed up or sinned against His commandments. No, He comes to us by the power of the Holy Spirit to gracefully convict us of our sins and then He waits patiently for us to see our wrong and to ask forgiveness then to turn from our wicked ways.

He is a loving Father who knows we are not perfect. He takes us as we are. His ultimate goal is for each of us to be transformed from glory to glory. To see the gift of His love and forgiveness through the death of His Son Jesus, then to be transformed to be like Him.

But, just as it is in writing you must be willing to be critiqued. You must be willing to take what you believe to be perfect and say to another, 'Find my flaws. Find what is in my work that will allow another to stumble as they read it." Only then can we get an honest opinion that will help others grow.

What about you --Do you see yourself as perfect? Are you willing to let the greatest author of all, sit down and read the story of your life as it is and make a few tweaks to perfect you for His Glory?

If you nodded yes, then maybe it's time. Present to Him your manuscript called life and see what His Spirit will reveal to you. Then sit in His Presence and allow Him to show you just what needs to be done to make you all He's destined you to be.

Prayer for the day: Oh Dear Jesus, You have created me. I am your workmanship. I sit today at Your feet and humbly ask You to show me where I have gone off the path and anything you would have me do or re-arrange in my life that I will be all You created me to be.

As you sit down with the Lord today, jot down what you feel He is speaking to your heart.

_____

_____

_____

_____

_____

_____

_____

_____

_____

_____

_____

_____

9

Gem Stones

*"However, as it is written: "What **no eye has seen**, what no ear **has** heard, and what no human mind **has** conceived"— the things God **has** prepared for those who love him—."*
1 Corinthians 2:9

God desires to bless His children with many beautiful treasures.

After the end of one of our Bible Studies, our group decided to meet for lunch since this was our final class. While we waited for our meal, one of the gals handed out a prayer rock to each of us. It was a small rock wrapped in a piece of material, tied with a ribbon and a cute little poem about prayer.

One of the ladies was curious what her rock looked like. As here curiosity got the best of her, she carefully untied the ribbon to peek inside. Everyone explained that it wasn't really meant to be opened, but her curiosity persisted. "Look," she said, "there's a cross on it! Right in the center

33

of my rock, there is a cross!"

Even though everyone had received one, Betty was the only one to persist and open it up and to see what was inside. The Word of God is similar to these little rocks. Although it was all wrapped up, Betty was persistent to see what was inside — and when she did, look at the excitement that was shared by all.

Shouldn't we be the same way? Excited to see what God has for us each day. The world has unknown things that we will face every day. Why not allow our curiosity get the best of us just like Betty and see what encouraging words of hope and wisdom the Lord has for us — Then when we do, we will be able to have His guidance and wisdom to carry us through our day.

I challenge you today to do like the rest of us finally did at our lunch, and untie the bow of your life to discover the wonderful treasures God has just for you.

Prayer for the day: Thank You Lord that Your desire is to bless us and to be with us throughout our day. May I open up to Your Word today and see what treasure You have for me.

As you sit down with the Lord today, jot down what you feel He is speaking to your heart.

_____

_____

_____

_____

_____

_____

_____

10

Grounded In Him

"I pray that out of His glorious riches He may strengthen you with power through His Spirit in your inner being, so that Christ may dwell in your hearts through faith. And I pray that you, being rooted and established in love, may have power, together with all the Lord's holy people, to grasp how wide and long and high and deep is the love of Christ."
Ephesians 3:16-18

Read Joshua 1: 1-7

Today while I was on my way to an appointment, I was unexpectedly delayed at a stop sign where I watched this freshly-grown oak tree being transported on a forklift.

I couldn't help but notice the deep roots dangling along. While I was sitting there, I envisioned that tree as our lives. We may appear to display a strong character on the outside, but what if the Lord decided to uproot us?

37

Would we wither away with just the thought of hearing the word relocation, or, are we rooted and grounded enough in Him to carry on no matter what? Would we be able to go forth, in faith, with all that we know that He has promised to do for us?

True peace is believing that we can bloom wherever we are planted. Remember, it's not about where we are, but Whose we are. Why not take a minute today and look within— Ask yourself, "How deep are my roots?" And not only how deep they are, but who or what are they grounded in?

Are they securely rooted in the Word of God and all the promises that God has for you, or, are they rooted in the things of this world? Only if they are grounded in the Word of God, will you be able to survive like that tree. Just as the storms from Mother Nature will threaten to uproot that tree, the storms of life will do the same for you.

So again, if the Lord decided to uproot you, could you survive? Are you rooted and grounded in Him to bloom wherever you are planted?

Prayer for the day: Oh Dear Jesus, I know that I am very comfortable where I am. I know I am not too excited when I hear the word *change*. Help me today to know that if it was Your choice to move me that You will always be with me, no matter where I go.

As you sit down with the Lord today, jot down what you feel He is speaking to your heart.

_____

_____

_____

_____

_____

_____

_____

_____

_____

_____

_____

_____

11

Hand in Hand

*"But he said to me, 'My **grace is sufficient** for you, for my power is made perfect in weakness.' Therefore, I will boast all the more gladly about my weaknesses, so that Christ's power may rest on me."*
2 Corinthians 12:9

God's grace extends beyond where we can go. When we believe that we have come to the end of our self, God's grace will always be there to pick us up. And not only will it pick us up, but it will also raise us up to a higher level. If we could make it through the difficulties on our own, we would not need His grace to help us through—nor would we need a measure of faith to believe He can do it. That's where faith and grace meet—it's not like you have to pick and choose; grace and faith go hand in hand.

About one year ago, I went through a battle with my health. It was something unexpected, but none the less, it was there. I needed the faith to believe I would be okay.

41

Night after night I would stay awake in fear that if I fell asleep, I would not awake in the morning.

But praise God, His grace brought me through. His grace was extended beyond where family and friends couldn't take me. Although they tried to encourage me, fear would rise in the wee hours of the morning and God would meet me there to calm my fears.

He gave me a particular phrase that I'd love to share with you. He said, "Grace meets you at the threshold of every door." So beloved, even though you're in the midst of something unthinkable—God has not forgotten you.

As we study the life of Paul, he desperately needed God's grace as he went forth to preach the gospel. Talk about being stressed; he was hard pressed on every side. Yet, he maintained a strong faith in the message of Jesus Christ—and whether imprisoned or free, he continued on. He went forth to preach the gospel and to plant churches wherever he went and also to write two third of the New Testament.

So, if you need a measure of God's grace today, believe it is readily available. Re-read the scripture verse for today and hold fast to the words that the Lord said to Paul when he asked for the thorn to be removed from his side, and then have the faith to believe that His grace will be sufficient for you.

Prayer for the day: Dear Jesus, when I read the story of Paul and all that he endured for You, how can I complain? I thank You today for his example of how You carried him through everything he did for You.

As you sit down with the Lord today, jot down what you feel He is speaking to your heart.

_____

_____

_____

_____

_____

_____

_____

_____

_____

_____

_____

_____

_____

12

He Knows Me By Name

"He will prepare a table for me in the presence of my enemies."
Psalm 23:5

I have worked in the restaurant business since I was sixteen years old. I learned how to balance a tray on my shoulder while serving with dignity and poise. I also spent time behind the scenes in the kitchen where I iced, sliced and even diced.

How well I remember many weekends when my sister, Annie, my mom, and I worked at a local hall where we catered numerous social functions. We decorated platters from appetizers to relishes trays and mouth-watering deserts. My favorite was Christmastime. We carefully placed Christmas cookies in a beautiful array to set among the holiday decorations upon the banquet tables.

A great deal time and patience went into every event. Balance, perfection, and continuity were all part of the make-up. Thinking back, I just realized that all the

45

preparations we made were for total strangers. We worked with such diligence even though we never knew names of those we served.

While reading Psalm 23 today, a thought crossed my mind. If all of the feasts that we had prepared with such perfection were for strangers, then what will God's banquet be like for us? He created me. He knows me by name. David tells us that God will prepare a feast for us in the presence of our enemies— could we even begin to imagine what the God who loves us so much would prepare for those who love Him?

Oh, beloved just stop for a minute and think about it. The God of the entire universe knows you by name. He not only knows you by name but He is aware of everything that you are experiencing right now. When the day comes that you see Him face to face, He will prepare the greatest and the most incredible banquet you could ever imagine!

Prayer for the day: Dear Heavenly Father, it amazes me beyond all human consumption to think that You know me by name and that You are concerned with everything I do. I know that I will never understand all until I sit at the banquet with You in eternity.

As you sit down with the Lord today, jot down what you feel He is speaking to your heart.

_____

_____

_____

_____

_____

_____

13

Hide n Seek

"He who dwells in the secret place of the Most High shall abide under the shadow of the Almighty. I will say of the Lord, He is my refuge and my fortress; My God, in whom I will trust."
Psalm 91: 1-2

Do you remember the childhood game of hide and seek? One person would cover their eyes and count to one-hundred while the others tried to find their favorite hiding place. Once everyone was out of sight, the person counting would yell out, "Ready or not here I come."

Well, sometimes in life, things seem to come after you the same way— but unannounced, "Here I come." Unexpectant things occur to you or someone you love. But it's not like when you were kids, and you'd get a warning— this is real, and it's called life.

If you led a sheltered life, it might seem all the more dramatic to you and difficult to handle. But if you grew up in a family where you were used to drama and chaos all the

49

time, then things that interfere might come naturally for you.

Whatever your situation is, things do happen. Unfortunate and unforeseen things will come our way, and the safest place to go when they arise, is right to the Lord. He is already aware of your circumstances. Like in the game, do you remember how safe you felt in your little hiding space—but yet, the anticipation of wondering just when they were going to find you?

You could hear the footsteps getting closer and closer and their voice getting louder and louder until the door quickly opened or the covers flew off. There you were. Your hiding place exposed, and you laughed and laughed till you cried.

Well, God wants you to know, that feeling of security still holds for you today. You don't need to hide under the bed, or back in the farthest part of your closet. No, God provides a different type of security for you. The Psalmist tells us, we can find comfort and protection under the shadow of the Almighty—and beloved, think of a shadow, it can be either in front of us or behind us depending where the light hits.

So hold fast and believe that if you need God in front of you, He will go before you. Or if you need Him behind, He will be there also—He will hold you up. The key today is to trust. Yes, trust and be assured that He will be there no matter what. Then and only then will we be able to experience that feeling of security no matter who shouts out, "Ready or not, here I come!"

Prayer for the day: Dear God, I know that I do not know what the future holds for me. But I thank You today that whatever happens that You will be there to protect me through it.

As you sit down with the Lord today, jot down what you feel He is speaking to your heart.

_____

_____

_____

_____

_____

_____

_____

_____

_____

_____

_____

_____

_____

_____

14

Home

"What is more, I consider everything a loss because of the surpassing worth of knowing Christ Jesus my Lord, for whose sake I have lost all things. I consider them garbage, that I may gain Christ and be found in him, not having a righteousness of my own that comes from the law, but that which is through faith in Christ."
Philippians 3:8-9

Read 2 Corinthians 4

For the past few years, my husband and I have been searching for a house. Our real estate agent tried to meet our needs. She took us out several times, but each time it just wasn't the right one.

Then one night while I was searching on the internet, I stumbled upon a listing for a move-in ready spec house that was holding an open house the very next day. It seemed to be just what we were looking for so after church we decided to scoot on over.

As we pulled into the drive, I said, "I think we found it…" Then before my husband even a stepped through the door, he said the exact same thing. Once inside, we both were amazed. It was perfect. Colors, décor and even the layout of the home was exactly what we wanted.

You see, just as the real-estate agent thought that she knew what we wanted – each house came short of our expectation. Well, the enemy thinks he knows what we need also. He throws many things our way. He tricks us into believing that the things of this world will give us pleasure and meet our needs, but God created each of us with a vacuum that only He can fill. We try to fill it with all the things of this world that we think will make us happy, but nothing actually sustains us until we find Him.

Just like trying to find the right house, we know when we have found our home in Christ. Beloved, since He is our Creator, He knows each of us personally. He also knows until we find the true meaning of salvation, and what Jesus did for each of us – and we ask Him to come in and take residence in our heart, nothing else will do.

God knows best. He doesn't have to think that He knows what we need. He knows that our peace and our hope can only be found in Jesus, Who offers us the hope of eternal life with Him.

Prayer for the day: Dear God, I have tried all the things of this world to satisfy myself. Although they lasted for a time, I always just felt empty inside. Thank you for providing Your Son, Jesus to bring me the peace, the love and the joy I can only find in Him.

As you sit down with the Lord today, jot down what you feel He is speaking to your heart.

_____

_____

_____

_____

_____

_____

_____

_____

_____

_____

_____

_____

15

Jesus Calling

*"Blessed is the one whose delight is in the law of the LORD,
and who meditates on his law day and night.
That person is like a tree planted by streams of water,
which yields its fruit in season
and whose leaf does not wither— whatever they do prospers."
Psalm 1:2*

Today we live in the world of computers. Like anything in the world, it can be used for good, or for bad. Because I live in a different state than my grandchildren, I choose to see the computer as something good. I praise God that there is a way of communing with them even if we're miles apart.

When my granddaughter Izabela first got her iPad, she would facetime me every morning. As soon as she would wake up, there she was. Sometimes she'd even call me while snuggled under her covers. Many times I'd be sound asleep, and her call would wake me right up. Even if I was barely

57

awake, I'd never deny my little granddaughter the chance to greet her and say good-morning.

That was about two years ago. We still Facetime now and then, but not as much as in the beginning. Although I miss her daily calls, I know that the newness has worn off; but not her love.

Many times when we first develop our relationship with the Lord it's the same way. We can't wait to get up and spend every waking hour with Him. We can't wait to delve right into His Word and see what He has for the day. Then, time elapses. Oh yes, we still love Him, and we still need Him, but things begin to sneak up somehow, and before we know it, they even get in the way.

Morning chores step in. Important e-mails need attention, and Facebook and Twitter might need a tweet-- And where is Jesus? Oh, He is still there waiting for us. He is right where He was the last time we spoke with Him.

Just like Izabela, yes, I do get to talk to her on the phone, and sometimes on the iPad, but sadly not as much as before. Although I know she still loves her grandma and cherishes every moment that we are together, I still miss those early risers.

…Jesus Calling… His love, His mercy, and His grace await you. He is there at this very moment just waiting for you. Waiting for you to turn off the phone. To shut down the computer, and open up your Bible to snuggle up with Him right now.

Prayer for the day: Dear Jesus, please forgive me. I do hear Your call. I am sorry that sometimes the things of the world seem to find their way to take me away from You. May I come and draw close to you today.

As you sit down with the Lord today, jot down what you feel He is speaking to your heart.

_____

_____

_____

_____

_____

_____

_____

_____

_____

_____

_____

_____

16

Jesus Where Are You?

"Lo, I am with you always, even to the end of the age."
Matthew 28:20

Did you ever have someone quote that scripture to you when you were going through a tough time? When it seemed like everything that came across your path was against you? When everyone else seemed to have the perfect life and yours was spinning out of control?

Sometimes it's not easy when we're facing an impossible situation to read and even to believe a scripture, especially one that says Jesus is with you. We feel like we've prayed our last prayer and we just don't know what to do. That's when we sit down and ask ourselves, "Jesus, where are you?"

Think of the disciples. They were the ones that Jesus said this to just before he ascended into heaven. He told them, *I am always with you, even till the end of the age.* Do you think they might have been confused? I do... and if someone was about to leave me and told me that they would always be with me, my mind would wonder. How? How can you be with me if you are going away?

Jesus was speaking to them in the spiritual sense. He knew that they would no longer be able to see him in the human form, but they would be able to reach him in the Spirit. He had not baptized them yet in the Holy Spirit when this comment was made, but He knew the future. He knew what would happen in the Upper Room when He would thunder down upon them with His Precious Holy Spirit to lead them and to guide them into all truth.

The good news is my beloved, that He did not only leave the Holy Spirit for the disciples, but he left Him for you and me. The Holy Spirit is there to lead and guide you today in that very situation you are in. Although you may feel like everything is spinning out of control, call upon Him. Take time to sit before the Lord and pour out your heart and your trouble to Him. Then allow the precious Holy Spirit of God to come in and minister to you as only He can do.

Prayer for the day: Dear Jesus, You know my situation. You know my inner fears and hurts. I thank you for giving me the promise that You will be with me till the end of the ages. Help me to remember that especially when I enter into troubled times.

As you sit down with the Lord today, jot down what you feel He is speaking to your heart.

_____

_____

_____

_____

_____

_____

_____

_____

_____

_____

_____

_____

_____

17

Love vs Wrath

The LORD said to Joshua, "Stand up! What are you doing down on your face? Israel has sinned; they have violated my covenant, which I commanded them to keep."
Joshua 7:10

I love the book of Joshua. But before I understood God's perfect love, I wouldn't go near the Old Testament. I only saw the wrath and anger of God towards His children. I didn't see that God is a loving God full of mercy and forgiveness. It's us who refuse to heed unto the word of God and sadly that is what turns His love into anger.

God directed Joshua step by step in taking Jericho. He told them to march around the city for seven days in silence while praising Him. If they did as He said, He promised that the walls would fall down and they would take the city.

They were obedient. They did as God said. God kept His promise and they seized Jericho. Sadly, the next battle was quite different. Joshua lost some of His men and he reacted by lying on his face asking the Lord why? As we read on, we find out that some of his men disobeyed God's covenant and took some of the accursed things from the previous battle. Therefore, they could not stand before their enemies.

God wants to be with us in our battles, like a loving parent who wishes to walk alongside their own children through their struggles in life. But when we disobey, we get in the way of the perfect relationship He desires to have with us. When a parent tells their child what to do, and the child disobeys, the parent doesn't stop loving that child, but it's very difficult not be become angry when your words have fallen upon deaf ears.

Beloved, could you be like Joshua today—on your face before God asking why your prayers have not been answered? Do you feel you are struggling in a never ending battle? Then, recall what God has told you and promised you in days before; and if you have done all he has commanded to do, then stand—Yes, stand and wait upon God to follow through with his promises to you.

If, on the other hand, God has spoken and you have disobeyed what God has directed, then get in His presence, repent before Him and trust and see what He will do in His appointed time.

Prayer for the day: Dear God search my heart. Search me today and let me know if there is anything You have spoken to me that I have failed to do. I thank You for not only your love but the loving way that You bring correction to me.

As you sit down with the Lord today, jot down what you feel He is speaking to your heart.

_____

_____

_____

_____

_____

_____

_____

_____

_____

_____

_____

_____

18

Melodies From The Heart

"Then the LORD called Samuel. Samuel answered, "Here I am Lord."
1 Samuel 3:4

Have you ever heard a song that brought you back to the exact time and place which triggered a memory from your past? Whenever I hear the song Ave Maria, I always think of my mom since it was one of her favorites.

One unforgettable memory I have from that song is when she was in the hospital. She had been on a respirator for about a week. Finally she regained her consciousness and was moved out of ICU. My brother Tony and I were the only ones in the room at that time.

He began to sing Ave Maria at her bedside. Now Tony is not just a ho-hum singer as I, he is truly gifted with a powerful voice that he uses for the Lord. As he started to sing, the tears began to roll down my face.

I went to the bathroom area to grab a tissue to dry my

eyes. I was surprised to see one of the housekeepers was standing there with tears welling up in hers. "Who—who is that singing?" she asked, "His voice— It's so beautiful."

I told her that it was my younger brother and that he was the choir director in his church, also, that he sang in church for most of his adult life. As she continued to wipe her eyes, she said only God knew that she needed to hear him today. "I'm not usually on this floor," she added through her tears, "but my supervisor sent me up here to clean this room today."

You see beloved, when we exercise the gifts that God has placed within us, it touches people we may never even know. Tony had no idea until he finished that he was ministering to one of the gals in the hospital—he just did what came naturally to him at that moment.

Sometimes we think that to do things for God, it must be great. It must be enormous— but when it's for Him, it can be speaking, or singing, teaching, or whatever He has called us to do, either to a crowd of thousands— or in this case, to an audience of one.

When we believe that there are so many hurting people in this world and that God needs each of us to go into His hurting world and bring a silhouette of joy or hope to them, then we can do it not to receive applause from men, but to bring glory to our Father in heaven.

Prayer for the day: Dear God, Here I am… Use me today wherever you might need me to go.

As you sit down with the Lord today, jot down what you feel He is speaking to your heart.

_____

_____

_____

_____

_____

_____

_____

_____

_____

_____

_____

_____

_____

19

Out of The Dumpster and Into His Word

"In him we have redemption through his blood, the forgiveness of sins, in accordance with the riches of God's grace that He lavished on us."
Ephesians 1:7

Have you ever had a time when you contemplated on a past mistake or wrong choice until every sentence started with, "What if?"

I think we've all been there and we know in our heart of hearts it's a dangerous place to be. It's a place where the enemy likes to take us, where we begin to focus on the mistakes of our past, and without even realizing it, we begin to take the focus off the promises of God. If we're not careful, that downhill spiraling can easily get out of control and steer us in the wrong direction.

Why live in the regret of the past when God has so much for us in our future? Scripture tells us that we have redemption through His blood. We have forgiveness of our sins. And not only the forgiveness of our sins but in accordance with the riches of God's grace that He lavished on us.

So, if His forgiveness, redemption, and His grace is lavished on us, why would we choose to dig way down into that dirty dumpster of our past and dig up some old ugly stuff then allow it to continue to have a hold on us.

Oh dear beloved, God has so much more for you. He wants to take you to greater and mightier things. He wants to bestow His love and His mercy upon you all the days of your life. He wants to take you to places you've never been. Places where you can experience His forgiveness and be able to become a mighty witness for Him to others who need to know of His love and mercy.

So, how about it? Let go of the past. Let go of the stinking thinking and begin to think in a whole new way. Begin to dive into the Word of God and discover the many promises that God has for you. Remember your future is at stake. Don't let the past continue to be a stronghold for you when you have a mighty fortress in your God. Allow the love and forgiveness and grace of Our Lord begin to take residence in you like never before.

Allow it to wash away that past once and for all that as soon as it tries to raise its ugly head again, you will be able to speak to it in the name of Jesus and command it to go back to where it came and never to haunt or taunt you again.

Prayer for the day: Oh Dear Jesus, I know You died for me. I know You have forgiven me of all my sins. I thank You today that You have redeemed me of my past mistakes and experiences and You truly desire new and good things for me. I thank You today for Your love and grace to help me experience all You have for me. Amen.

As you sit down with the Lord today, jot down what you feel He is speaking to your heart.

_____

_____

_____

_____

_____

_____

_____

_____

_____

_____

_____

_____

_____

20

Pass The Mercy Please

"For the wages of sin is death, but the gift of God is eternal life in
Christ Jesus our Lord."
Romans 6:23

I grew up in a family with three brothers and two sisters—you better believe there was always something going on. One of the things we loved to do as kids was to have tickle fights. With one pinned to the ground, the others would tickle till they just couldn't take it anymore and suddenly the cry of mercy rang throughout our tiny living room.

Pleading for mercy—sounds a bit like life when we feel we're pinned down because of poor choices we've made. We know that we had a choice in the matter, but for whatever the reason, we made the wrong one. Rather than do what was right, we went the other way. Just like when we were kids, we knew the joy/pain of getting on the

77

ground for the others to anxiously attack, but we did it anyway.

Then when the pain was too severe, mercy called out. As children of our heavenly Father, we can do the same. We know that the wages of our sin is death, but through the death of His Son Jesus, who willing laid down *His* life for us, mercy is granted. The sin that has tainted our lives, brought guilt and shame, can now be forgiven through the cross.

Although Our Father God knew we would sin— He knew we would mess up yet He provided a way out. He provided a pardon for our sin through the death of His Son, Jesus.

So beloved, if you feel like this word is for you, and you just can't take it anymore and sin has you pinned to the ground, maybe it's time to give up. Yes, time to repent of your sins and cry out for this mercy that only He can give.

Believe that your heavenly Father has waited for this moment for the longest time. Let today be the first day of the rest of your life. Allow the guilt and shame to be washed away by the precious blood of Jesus and allow the mercy of God to rule and reign in your life and your heart forever.

Prayer for the day: Oh Father God, I do want this new life in You. Help me to humble myself today, to repent of my sins and to receive the gift of the mercy that You have waiting just for me. I thank You for standing before me, ready and willing to forgive.

As you sit down with the Lord today, jot down what you feel He is speaking to your heart.

_____

_____

_____

_____

_____

_____

_____

_____

_____

_____

_____

_____

_____

21

Push On

"I can do all through Christ who strengthens me."
Philippians 4:13

Every year we experience changes in our bodies; and sometimes, actually most of the time, it's maybe a little more than we would like. For some reason everything tends to fall. I guess it's the law of gravity. What goes up must come down.

Today while talking to my son Brian, I was surprised with the question he asked, "Are you still working out Mom? Are you taking care of yourself?" he added. Actually I can't say I answered yes to everything, but I do what I can, when I can.

"Mom," he added, "When you do work out and use your weights, remember what I told you to do. When you finish your reps, add another five pounds and do five more, then add five more and push yourself to do one or even two. By doing this you will stretch your muscles and strengthen them more and more each day."

Interesting concept and really, isn't that what faith is all about? Faith is trusting God no matter what. Especially when we are facing something that seems impossible -- we must trust Him all the more. We must *choose* to remember what God has carried us through in the past and then stand and believe that if He has done it before, He can do it again.

Think about adding that extra weight to strengthen our muscles. Battles and unforeseen circumstances are just like adding extra weight to our already chaotic life – so instead of feeling powerless when that extra weight is laid upon you, try to push yourself to believe. Maybe read an old journal or do something to that will help you remember all that He has done for you in the past.

Linking the past to your present circumstance will in turn strengthen your faiths in time of need. Also, remember to stand on His promises. Get in the habit of repeating positive scripture out loud – hear yourself decree and declare what you can do and also God's promises for you. Today's scripture is a perfect one to keep in you sight, "I *can do all through Him that strengthens me.*" And, beloved, the next time you face another problem, remember He did it before and He will do it again

Prayer for the day: Dear God, I know that You are in every battle that I face. Help me to remember that my faith is a muscle. Help me to exercise it every day in every circumstance that comes my way.

As you sit down with the Lord today, jot down what you feel He is speaking to your heart.

_____

_____

_____

_____

_____

_____

_____

_____

_____

_____

_____

_____

_____

22

See Weeds?

"Search me, O God, and know my heart; test me and know my anxious thoughts."
Psalm 139: 23

Read Psalm 139

As I walked the beach one morning, I enjoyed the peace and tranquility of the ocean. I watched her mighty waves crash upon the shore then gently recede to her ever-flowing body of water.

Continuing on, I noticed patches of seaweed that was brought up from the depth of the sea. How could such muck and guck live beneath this beautiful span of water?

With that thought, I began to think of our lives. Many of our peers see us as well kept—all together, let's say they see us from the outside in, not vice versa. But God, and only God can see what is there. He knows the muck and guck we hold on to from the past. Sometimes it can even be things all the way back from our childhood like hurt or pain or even shame from things that we had no control over.

Only when we give Him permission will He be able to help us. He stands ready and able—but we must be the ones to surrender. Once we do, He will send the Holy Spirit, His precious Holy Spirit, who will gently guide us to search the hidden chambers of our mind and uncover what is there. Then, with everything exposed, we will be able to face our past—good and bad—and finally, be liberated from anything that has entangled us within.

Just like the ocean—only when the tide rushes in, is the seaweed brisk fully carried to the shore and brought in to be laid bare to the ground. As the muck and guck is left behind, the freshly clean water gently recedes back to her ever-flowing body of water.

Why not allow the tide of the Holy Spirit to rush in today and reach you right where you are? Allow Him to help rid your soul of anything that may be keeping you from all that God has for you?

Then, my beloved, when you are free of all that has held you captive, you will be free to walk in the peace, love, and joy that God has always destined for you.

Prayer for the day: Dear God, as each wave returns to its ever-flowing body of water, so shall I return to You. Today, I give permission for Your, Holy Spirit, to peer deep within and reveal anything that has been holding me back from being all I can be in You.

As you sit down with the Lord today, jot down what you feel He is speaking to your heart.

_____

_____

_____

_____

_____

_____

_____

_____

_____

_____

_____

_____

_____

23

Signed, Sealed and Delivered

"Trust in the Lord with all your heart, lean not on your
own understanding; but in all your ways acknowledge Him
And He will direct your path."
Proverbs 3:5

Today I wrote a letter, tucked it into an envelope, sealed it closed and without hesitation and dropped it into a huge blue mailbox. Walking away I thought, *that was an important letter, I sure hope it doesn't get lost.*

In the little town where I live, there are about 20,000 residents. Imagine if one day, every single person mailed just one letter; how many letters would be? How can I be assured that my one envelope will find it's way through the heaps and heaps of mail?

I can't, but I must trust. The same as I must trust for this simple letter on a greater magnitude is how we need to trust God with every day problems. When facing a difficulty, we are told to give it to God and lay it at the cross then go on believing in faith that He will take care of it.

But just like the letter, once released, we walk away doubting. But just because we doubt it doesn't mean that we will reach back into the mailbox and then deliver it ourselves. So why when we present our problems to God do we feel the need to reach back and take things into our own hands?

As the scripture tells us, lean *not* on our own understanding. When we lean on our own understanding, the first thing we do is to try and figure out the solution. In all reality, that's the thing we cannot do. Sometimes things are so far out of our control, that the only thing we can possibly do is to trust that God has the answer and the means greater than we can think or even imagine.

Let today be the beginning of a new day. Realize that if we can trust the postal system through rain or shine, how much easier our lives will be when we honestly learn to trust God, Our Heavenly Father with every thing we face.

Prayer For The Day: Dear Heavenly Father thank You for being there for me. I ask today for the courage to learn to trust all my needs and wants with You.

As you sit down with the Lord today, jot down what you feel He is speaking to your heart.

_____

_____

_____

_____

_____

_____

_____

_____

_____

_____

_____

_____

24

Smooth Out The Scratches, Jesus

"Therefore, putting away lying, "Let each one of you speak the truth with his neighbor, for we are members of one another. Be angry, and do not sin, do not let the sun go down on your wrath, nor give place to the devil."
Ephesians 4 25-27

Anger can lead to sin.

In today's scripture, Paul tells us not to let the sun go down on our wrath. Anger is like cancer. Sometimes it can be prevented if it is detected early enough—unfortunately, sometimes it may be too late. Anger resulting from harsh words or actions of another can have the same effects on our physical and spiritual life. You see when we carry angry thoughts or words with us, the scene of what happened continues to replay over and over like a broken record.

Does anyone remember those LP's or 45's? When a song was stuck, it would play over and over till someone lifted the arm off the record and moved it beyond. 'Beyond what?' Beyond the scratch—most of the times it was a tiny scratch impossible for the human eye to see—that caused the record to keep on playing.

We walk around with scratches in our life and sometimes even upon our heart because of a hurt that was so deep that we just can't let go. Like that record, we just allow the words, the scene to play over and over again.

Today, take it to Jesus. Ask Him to help you deal with it. Simply lay it at the foot of the cross and allow His love and mercy to help you heal.

Sometimes, He might lead you to connect with that person who has hurt you and make amends—and other times, He might simply direct you to let it go and allow Him to work it out as only He can do—However He directs you, trust that He has seen all from beginning to end, and He knows what is best.

Then, beloved, once the scratches in your life are smoothed out, you will be able to regain the spirit of peace and joy which will allow His love and mercy to flow out through you to be able to forgive others just the same as Jesus has done for you.

Prayer for the day: Dear God, help me to let go feelings of anger or hate that I have harbored inside. I know that things stored up in darkness only continue to grow. Let me open wide the windows of my soul that I will hear from You, and then be able to forgive and forget as You direct me to do.

As you sit down with the Lord today, jot down what you feel He is speaking to your heart.

———————————————————————

———————————————————————

———————————————————————

_____

_____

_____

_____

_____

_____

_____

_____

_____

25

Spirit Sense

"All this I have spoken while still with you. But the Counselor, the Holy spirit, whom the Father will send in my name, will teach you all things and will remind you of everything I have said."
John 14:25

Haste makes waste!

What a great word to keep us on track. I can remember many times when my mom would use that phrase to get one of us, kids to slow us down.

Although that was some time ago, and she's gone on to glory, I still hear those three words ringing loud and clear when I try to juggle too many things at one time— "Del, go ahead," I can hear her say, "but you'll find out that your haste will make waste!"

Jesus carries on a very important conversation with his disciples in John 14 and John 15. He's trying to bring comfort to them as He explains that He will not be with

97

them much longer. Jesus tells them that even though He must leave, His Father in heaven would send them another counselor—The Holy Spirit who would be with them forever.

As we read on, we can see that He even tells them to have peace. He knows, with the news of His departure, that they would begin to fear. He also knew that the Holy Spirit would be there every day to encourage them and teach them in his absence.

One of the most important things that we can learn from today's scripture is that the same Holy Spirit that was left for the disciples is available for us today. He is a person. He is the third person of the Trinity and a person is more than just a word. He is there to speak to us when we need encouragement—when we are in trouble—when we have an important decision to make—He is there for us.

Just like my mom was there to alert the six of us, kids, about rushing along, the Holy Spirit is there to lead and guide us into all truth. Beloved, all you need to do is to call upon Him. Ask Him for His help and then listen for His still small voice to speak.

Prayer for the day: Dear Father God, I thank You for the gift of Your Precious Holy Spirit. Help me to remember that in time of need, or comfort, or direction He is only a word away.

As you sit down with the Lord today, jot down what you feel He is speaking to your heart.

_____

_____

_____

_____

_____

_____

_____

_____

_____

_____

_____

_____

26

Splash of Beauty

"Seek first His kingdom and His righteousness and all these things will be given to you as well."
Matthew 6:33

A few weeks ago, my husband and I attended a community luncheon. During the meal, I admired the colorful array of flowers on each table. When it was over, I thought, *I wish I could take just one of those pinkish tulips home with me.*

Later on, that evening, when we arrived home from a church service, we noticed a vase of flowers at our front door. *Who were they from?* We soon discovered that the flowers were a thank you from the coordinator of our noon luncheon, in return for tablecloths that I allowed her to use.

"God is awesome!" I exclaimed. "I would have been happy with just one tulip, and yet He gave me the whole roomful."

God is that way. We all have wants and needs.

Sometimes it's a bit of a struggle as we try to acquire them on our own. In doing so, we are forgetting that God's resources are much greater than we can ever begin to imagine.

When we begin to discover the heart of God, we realize that He desires to give us more than we could ever want or imagine. As our heavenly Father, He longs to fulfill our heart's desire. Take time today and meditate on this verse in Matthew. Jesus tells us to seek first the kingdom of God and all else will be established. He is telling us that God does not want us to worry about tomorrow. Just seek Him and trust Him because He was in yesterday, He is in today and He will also be there in your tomorrow.

When we truly begin to seek Him with all our heart, the desires of the world fall away. Yes, the needs of the world and the things that we need to sustain us in our daily lives will still be there, but it's our heart's desires that begin to change.

He knows what lies deep within our hearts and when our focus is more on Him and the ways of His kingdom, he delights then in giving us the desires of our heart and to meet our needs in ways we can't even begin to imagine.

So my beloved, the next time you begin to think small, enlarge your vision and see what God will do for you.

Prayer for the day: Dear God, I know that you always have my best in mind. Help me to learn to focus more on You. I thank You today and You stand waiting to meet my earnest hearts desires.

As you sit down with the Lord today, jot down what you feel He is speaking to your heart.

_____

_____

_____

_____

_____

_____

_____

_____

_____

_____

_____

_____

27

Take It To The Lord

"And it came to pass in these days that He went out into the mountain to pray; and he continued all night in prayer to God."
Luke 6:12

Are you looking for answers? Do you fear many of the things going on in our world today? Do you need help with broken relationships? If so — *Take it to The Lord.*

I can remember before my husband and I were married, I would ask him a question about particular worries I had, or direction I needed in my life, and he would always give me the same answer — Take it to the Lord. Many times I would get frustrated because I really wanted him to help guide me at that moment, but he'd always respond the same. What I couldn't see back then was that he was helping me to develop my prayer life — *although I thought* it was pretty good, he enabled it to get stronger.

Just like a muscle, the more we exercise it, the stronger it becomes. Well, prayer is nothing more than having a conversation with God. And how can we develop a prayer life if we do not continually converse with Him?

One day, as I listened to a teaching on prayer, I heard a phrase that I often quote when I'm trying to give someone encouragement — don't go to the phone, go to the throne!

Good word. In our scripture today, we read that Jesus prayed all night to His Father, Why? Reading on, we see that the very next morning He chose His twelve disciples. So If Jesus went to His Father all night to pray before making such an important decision, then shouldn't we do the same?

Prayer is what moves the Father's hand. It compels His heart. He waits in expectation for us to converse with Him and to take our hurts and our cares to Him. 1Peter 5:7 says, *"Cast all your anxiety on him because he cares for you."*

So beloved there is nothing more dependable to stand on. Our heavenly Father truly does care for you so deeply and everything that pertains to you and our loved ones. When we truly come to believe that and understand it, why then would we not first and foremost stand in faith, and — *Take it to The Lord!*

Prayer for the day: Dear Heavenly Father, I know that there is nothing too big for You. There is nothing going on in this world that is a surprise to You either, You have seen it from beginning to end, so today I make a decision to begin my prayer life with You and to come to You each day, and all throughout the day when something arises that I need You to help me with.

As you sit down with the Lord today, jot down what you feel He is speaking to your heart.

_____

_____

_____

_____

_____

_____

_____

_____

_____

_____

_____

_____

_____

28

The Great Divide

*"For this reason Christ is the mediator of a new covenant, that
those who are called may receive the promised eternal
inheritance—now that he has died as a ransom to set them free
from the sins committed under the first covenant."*
Hebrews 9:15

Do you ever think about your childhood days? What
would you say is your fondest memory from grade school?

Mine would be math. How I loved multiplication, but
oh how I hated division. I guess I just didn't like the fact
that something had to be divided up.

That brings to mind today, *The Great Divide*—what is it,
really? Roughly it is two thousand eight hundred miles
between Canada and Mexico which split the North
American continent in two. Many people use the expression
to relate it to numerous things in life—friendships, sports
teams, political parties, and even divorce.

People have written songs about it, made documentaries

explaining it, and still, others have written novels pertaining to it—but what would the greatest divide of ever truly be?

What about God? How frightening for the Great Divide to be a separation from God for all eternity. Imagine being cut off, disconnected from your Heavenly Father forever and ever—never being able to call out His name and know that He would come to your aid.

Oh but beloved, not one of us need to go there. God in His great love and mercy has created a way out for each of us. As His Son, Jesus, laid down His life for us, that was His way of bridging that gap through all eternity.

The writer of Hebrews tells us that Christ is the mediator of a New Covenant, that those who are called may receive the promised eternal inheritance—now that He has died as a ransom to set them free from the sins. (*Hebrews 9:15*).

The precious blood of Jesus that was shed on that cross over two thousand years ago was shed as the final sacrifice for all—yes, the ultimate sacrifice to open the gates of heaven, for all who ask forgiveness of their sin committed under the first covenant shall one-day go in.

Prayer for the day: Dear Jesus, thank You for bridging the great divide by laying Your life down for me. As Hebrews 10:22 says, "May I draw near to You with a sincere heart in full assurance of faith, having my heart sprinkled to cleanse me from a guilty conscience and having my body washed with pure water."

As you sit down with the Lord today, jot down what you feel He is speaking to your heart.

_____

_____

_____

_____

_____

_____

_____

_____

_____

_____

_____

_____

_____

29

The Master Builder

"For I know the plans I have for you," declares the LORD, "plans to prosper you and not to harm you, plans to give you hope and a future."
Jeremiah 29:11

Read Psalm 139

During the time my husband and I were house hunting, we decided to check out a community of new homes in our area. Bernie, the sales rep, asked us if we'd like to see one of his new homes that was already under construction. As we responded yes, he carefully led us around the skeletal walls of a soon- to- be- built home. It didn't take long for us to get a picture of just how beautiful the finished project would be.

Psalm 139 tells us that we are wonderfully knit in our mother's womb. The choice of words that the psalmist uses, knit, in our mother's womb, denotes how much care was taken to create us. If you've ever knitted or watched someone knit, then you know that it takes a lot of time and patience.

It is performed loop by loop with one continuous thread. We were made likewise; very carefully inch by inch by our heavenly Father. And, although we too are a mere skeletal being at that point, God has plans for a future and a great hope for us. Jeremiah 29 tells us that they are *"Plans to prosper you and not to harm you, plans to give you a hope and a future."*

When we learn to walk closely with The Lord, we can understand the plans that He has for us. Just like my husband and I, as we sat in the sales office with Bernie, he explained every aspect of the home and the wonderful amenities the community had to offer.

Sitting still with our heavenly Lord, the architect of our lives, will enable us to see all that He has for us.

Prayer for the day: Dear Father God, I Thank You that by Your loving- kindness I am wonderfully made. I believe that You hold the blueprint of my life in your hand. Teach me to walk ever so close with You so that I may know the destiny and the plans You have for me.

As you sit down with the Lord today, jot down what you feel He is speaking to your heart.

_____

_____

_____

_____

_____

_____

30

The Potter's Wheel

"Yet you, LORD, are our Father. We are the clay; you are the
potter*; we are all the work of your hand."*
Isaiah 64:8

Do you remember Play-Doh? Can you remember the hours that would slip away as you created something awesome only to mash it up into a ball, then to roll it out again and again to re-create another masterpiece?

I can recall how much fun we had as kids whereby every stretch of the imagination was alive and free. I think what I loved most of all was the smell when a brand new can was opened —actually not *just* the smell, but the way it felt so soft in my hand.

Although it generated hours of fun, after a while the dough would become coarse and difficult to use. Not only would it become hard, but sometimes it would begin to crumble, and guess what—it was ready for the trash.

Sound a bit like life? Maybe we feel like we've been used

117

and abused emotionally that we're so weighed down and that everything seems to be crumbling around us? Like you just can't take it anymore? That if someone doesn't come in and rescue you, you're just going to crash?

Well, I have good news for you today, take heart. God has something great for you right around the corner. Although you may feel like those crumbs of Play-Doh, and maybe like you're even ready for the trash, God in His loving mercy— in His loving kindness—in His loving grace is there to pick you up ever so gently, to place you in the palm of His hand and to lovingly mold you and shape you… body, soul, mind and spirit.

He sees everything going on around you. He hears your heart's cry in the dead of night. He knows your hurt and even your loneliness. How we praise Him, dearly beloved, that even when we are at the end of our rope, or we feel that we are of no good to others that we are always worth something to Him. Let us praise our Lord that He is the potter and that He is anxiously waiting to mend us and to mold us for His glory.

Prayer for the day: Dear Father God, I know that You are the potter and I am the clay, Today I thank You as you place me on Your potter's wheel to mend me and mold me for Your glory.

As you sit down with the Lord today, jot down what you feel He is speaking to your heart.

_____

_____

_____

_____

_____

_____

_____

_____

_____

_____

_____

_____

_____

31

The Ultimate Sacrifice

Read Hebrews 10

*"We have been made holy through the sacrifice of the body of
Jesus Christ once for all."*
Hebrews 10:10

Recently, my husband and I battled our insurance
company in a week-long trial to collect for a past loss.
Numerous times just as the witness was about to answer a
question that would reveal the truth, the opposing lawyer
would abruptly stand up and say, "I object, irrelevant!"

The judge responded in one of two ways. Either he'd
say, "Overruled," which allowed the witness to answer the
question, or he would simply say, "Abstain," which
prohibited the witness from answering at all.

The writer of Hebrews assures us of a different case
scenario when we stand before the ultimate judge, the final
judge when our days are through. No one will say, "Guilty."

No one will say, "I object," And most of all—no one will say, "Irrelevant."

Jesus did it all. He cleared the way. Our debt, regardless of our sins, if He truly is Lord of our life, has been paid. Jesus suffered a death that He did not deserve. Upon that hill, on Calvary, he took upon Himself the sins of the entire world. He took upon Himself your sins and mine.

As it also says in Hebrews twelve that Jesus is the author and perfecter of our faith, who for the joy set before Him endured the cross (Heb. 12:2). Our part is to come to believe in what He did and to repent of our sins and make Him Lord of our life.

When we choose to do this, an inner change will take place. Things that were important will become irrelevant and our hopes, our dreams, and our needs will be *in* Him and *for* Him.

What a gift it is to be made holy through Him. We are not holy in our own righteousness. We are only holy and able to live a holy life by what He has done for us.

Prayer for the day: Dear Jesus, as I read these scriptures today, open my eyes that I might truly see the price that You paid for me. I thank you for all that You have suffered that I might be with You for all eternity.

As you sit down with the Lord today, jot down what you feel He is speaking to your heart.

_____

_____

_____

_____

_____

_____

_____

_____

_____

_____

_____

_____

_____

32

The Uninvited Guest

"As she stood behind him at his feet weeping, she began to wet his feet with her tears. Then she wiped them with her hair, kissed them and poured perfume on them."
Luke 7:38

The stage is set. A Pharisee named Simon invites Jesus for dinner. An unexpected guest arrives. The presence in the room overtakes her as she crosses the threshold. Although she can't even see His face, she is overwhelmed by His Holiness. Shadows of her past creep into her mind. Her sins are before her and she begins to weep.

Standing behind Jesus, the first tear falls. Unaware of her whereabouts, she makes her way around him and falls to her knees. The second tear streams forth. It splashes upon His feet. Then another and another till his feet are saturated with her tears.

The aroma of the dinner is overtaken by the silence in the air. She continues to weep then gracefully lets down her long dark hair as a means to dry her master's feet. Next, she opens her once clenched fist to remove the tiny cap from the alabaster jar she held tightly within her hand. The fragrance of the expensive perfume now permeates the room as she allows this once savored oil to now flow freely upon her master's feet.

Yes, the stage was set for this sinful woman to receive forgiveness of her sins that day. And so my beloved, it is the same for you and me as we approach the time of preparation of the Eucharist each Sunday. Will it really be possible to recall the words of this story ever again and just sit as usual as the Body of Christ is being prepared for us? How could we not fall to our knees in all humility knowing who is entering the room? How could His holiness not overtake us as it did with her that we too, can intimately present our sins to Jesus where we will hear Him say, "Your sins are forgiven. Your faith has saved you; go in peace."

Prayer for the day: Oh Dear Jesus, I, too, am a sinner just as this woman was. I want to be forgiven of my sins just like her. I confess to You that I am a sinner and I ask forgiveness of my sins. I fall at Your feet in all humility and thank You for Your life, Your death, and the gift of eternal life in You.

As you sit down with the Lord today, jot down what you feel He is speaking to your heart.

_____

_____

_____

_____

_____

33

The Way

"I am the way and the truth and the light
No one comes to the Father but through me."
John 14:6

What a comfort it must have been for the disciples when Jesus was explaining to them the way to heaven. We are so blessed that two thousand years later, the same applies to us.

To be able to visit a place you've never been, you would need a map to find your way. I remember our insurance company years ago had a program where they would completely map out your trip.

I know that I am dating myself a bit, but I believe it was called a TripTik. Page by page they would guide you with a red magic marker right from your front door to the desired destination. In our computerized generation, we have apps on our phone, in our car, and even on our iPads that do the same thing. Just type in where you are and then the address of where you want to go, and as soon as you hit start, this unidentified voice joins you on your journey and directs you turn by turn.

And—if you dare change your mind and take a more familiar route for part of the trip, or you stop for lunch or gas, she will blurt out, "Return to the designated route!" If you don't turn around immediately, she gets pretty huffy and repeats it over and over until you do.

Life's journey also has a map for us to follow. It's called the Bible. It is the greatest road map for our daily life that we can ask for. Within the Bible, we learn that Jesus paved the way for us. He paved our way to eternity. Yes, He took a journey that should have been ours.

He took the road that led to the cross where He was crucified and shed his blood for our sins. What a precious gift He gave for each of us. Why did He do this? He did it out of love. Pure, unselfish, unconditional love; He gave Himself as the sacrifice for our sins upon that cross.

Just the same way as the red marker directed the route that guided us along, the blood of Jesus maps our way when we believe in Him as Our Lord and Savior. When we confess our sins, that He is the way, and the truth and the life, He promises us eternal life with Him.

Prayer for the day: Dear Jesus, I will never understand how You could have suffered and died just for me. I am humbled that even if I was the only person on this earth, You would have still paved the way for me.

As you sit down with the Lord today, jot down what you feel He is speaking to your heart.

_____

_____

_____

_____

_____

_____

_____

_____

_____

_____

_____

_____

_____

34

To God Be the Glory

"So whether you eat or drink or whatever you do, do it all for the glory of God."
1 Corinthians 10:31

Kids have a mind of their own.

The other day, while I was at my daughter's house, I wanted to vacuum the kitchen floor. My grandson, Vincenzo thought it would be fun to help—since he's only a year old, I thought how am I going to handle this one. Besides the fact that he *couldn't* do it on his own, there was simply no way of saying no to him.

After trying to explain to 'why' he couldn't do it— and a few screeches later, I did what any powerless grandma would do; I let him help. Standing behind him and with my hands on the upper part of the vacuum, I allowed him to believe that he won the battle. Now and then he'd turn his cute little head and look up at me as if to say, "See Grandma, I can do it all by myself."

God knows that there are times that we are just like that. We see something that needs to be done in the Kingdom, and quickly we step out to do it. Sometimes we are qualified, and sometimes either we are not spiritually ready, or we just might need His help.

Because we believe we can do it, we go forth and get involved in different things for the Lord. Then when things don't go as we expected they would, or it's taking longer than we thought it should, frustration sets in. Sometimes we even say, "But Lord, I'm doing this for you, aren't I?"

We needed His help from the beginning. But sometimes we forget to pray and invite Him in. God can open mighty doors when we step out to do work in His Kingdom. Things that would in the natural take us forever, He can supernaturally complete in and instant.

God has put the gifts inside of us. And He is there like a Loving Father to lead and to guide us with all the necessities that we need to use these gifts to fulfill His purpose on the earth.

He knows the needs of his hurting people. So He calls us forth as The body of Christ to help and to equip others—when we ask for His help, we will always be able to accomplish what He desires us to do.

Prayer for the day: Dear God, I know that this world is full of hurting people. There is much work we can do for You. Please lead me and guide me with the gifts You have placed within me to use in Your kingdom.

As you sit down with the Lord today, jot down what you feel He is speaking to your heart.

_____

_____

_____

_____

_____

_____

_____

_____

_____

_____

_____

_____

_____

35

Too Close To Sea

"The Lord your God will be with you wherever you go."
Joshua 1:9

Vacation Bible School is always a challenge. One Sunday, Janice and I spent hours after service attempting to transform our youth room into an underwater adventure.

With an armload of plastic garment bags and a pack of green construction paper, we were ready. "Do you have any idea how we're going to do this?" Janice asked. "No…" I responded. "But just like last year, we'll just play around and let the creative juices flow and stand in awe to see what the Lord will do."

With a six-foot ladder and a reel of fishing wire, we managed to hang the ocean-blue plastic bags against the entire wall to create the effect we needed. Next, as I sat on the floor, I scooted myself along, to weave in bits of torn construction paper to create the wavering seaweed. Not sure if this would really work, I just kept on going.

Once I reached the end, I stood back in amazement. "Janice," I said, "How interesting. When I was sitting on the floor, and right on top of the project, I really couldn't see what I was doing at all. But when I stood back and looked at it—it actually looks like the ocean."

Isn't that just like our lives? When we are going through a difficult situation, and we are so entangled in it, we can't see anything but the problem. Sometimes we even feel like God's forgotten all about us. But as time goes on, and we begin to look back at that very instance, we not only see that He was right there with us, but how perfectly He was guiding us along.

Things we couldn't see when we were on top of them suddenly began to take on a new perspective. Many times, even today, when I'm just scooting along and stressed with the cares of this world, I look back upon that day. I remember that it wasn't until I stopped and looked back at the entire picture that I began to feel joy. A joy which causes me, even today, to pause and once again remember that not only is God here, but He's busy at work weaving everything in and out for His glory.

Prayer: Dear Father God, thank You for always being there. I know how many times I grow weary and impatient thinking that You've forgotten all about me. But today I thank You that no matter what I'm going through, You are right there.

As you sit down with the Lord today, jot down what you feel He is speaking to your heart.

_____

_____

_____

_____

_____

_____

_____

_____

_____

_____

_____

_____

_____

36

Under Construction

"My brethren count it all joy when you fall into various trials
knowing that the testing of your faith produces patience."
James 1:1

One of the roads that we travel quite frequently has been under construction for several months. You can imagine the inconvenience. One day it's everyone over to the left, and the next day, everyone over to the right. Beautiful landscaping has been transformed to mountains of dirt and traffic jams are a given during rush hour traffic. Although we know in the end it'll be to our advantage, it's still difficult to deal with right now.

So, the question of the day: "God, what do you want me to learn from this?" In times when I'm not really in a hurry, it doesn't bother me that much, but when I'm trying to get somewhere quick or I'm running late, the only thing to do is to practice patience.

How difficult is that to learn? In our fast paced world

with every electronic gadget available, patience can sometimes be averted. They have all the means to keep us instantly connected. But what about the times when something just comes up. Like when the construction worker holds up that orange sign that says, "stop," and you're fifteen minutes late already.

It's a given that things *will* happen in our life that we have no control over. Sickness, death, finances, and even job-related instances. If we've never had the opportunity to learn patience, then how do we handle it when we must? Oh, blood pressure rises, palms get sweaty and anger reaches its height, and the list goes on. Our scripture today gives us direction for such times as this. "Count it all joy," James says.

Yes, joy he said and I know it's a bit of an oxymoron, isn't it? *But it's only in finding joy in something that we have no control over that will keep us in perfect peace.*

Only when we have small trials such as these torn up roads to deal with, and we are forced to slow down and to ask God to give us the grace to help us through—because we know that eventually there will always be another trial on the way.

So beloved, let us learn to practice patience in the unimportant things like road blocks, so when the major things that are much more serious happen, we will be able to master it well; with God's grace and with Joy!

Prayer for the day: Dear God. You know it's so difficult to be patient. I ask You today for the grace that only You can give to help me in all times of my life when unforeseen trials come my way.

As you sit down with the Lord today, jot down what you feel He is speaking to your heart.

_____

_____

_____

_____

_____

_____

_____

_____

_____

_____

_____

_____

37

Under Cover

Read Ephesians 6 10-16

"Be sober; be watchful; because your adversary the devil walks about as a roaring lion, seeking whom he may devour."
1 Peter 5:8

One day, while I was sitting in the dentist chair, the dentist worked on my tooth to cover it with a crown. He lifted the temporary crown in and out numerous times, until it was good and tight. Whenever he placed it over the tooth, I was okay, but whenever he removed it, the cool air would hit my exposed gums and I'd dig my fingers deep into the chair and hold on for dear life.

To escape the pain, I prayed. It was then that I started to relate what was happening in my mouth and its similarities to a spiritual battle. Daily, we are faced with temptations. But being made of flesh, we are weak, and sometimes we fall into sin and become decayed like that tooth.

So, what do we do to protect ourselves to be able to withstand the temptation before us? Paul explains in Ephesians six; put on the full armor of God. He explains that the battles that continue to rage before us are not of flesh and blood, but against the forces of evil working in this world.

Starting with the top, he directs us to put on the helmet of salvation—this is to protect our mind, our eyes, our ears and anywhere that temptations can come in. Then, he tells us to put on the belt of truth; the truth that Jesus *is* our Lord and Savior, and He *is* the one to help us through any battle we face. Then with that belt tightly around our waist, He says to stand. To stand in that truth of who we are with the breastplate of righteousness covering our most vulnerable organ, the heart—where the enemy would love to wound us and then keep us bound.

Next is the shield of faith which will enable us to extinguish the fiery darts of the enemy and then stand with the sword of the Spirit which is the Word of God. Finally, beloved, and so very important, we must walk in peace. Paul encourages us to shod our feet with the gospel of peace and continue therefore to walk in it.

As you begin this as a daily regime to armor yourself piece by piece, you too will receive a crown as I. Oh, not as I over an infected tooth, but an eternal crown of life for all eternity.

Prayer for the day: Dear Father God, we know that the enemy stands waiting to devour us each and every day. Thank You for enabling us to be able to gird ourselves Your armor to protect us from, all that comes our way.

As you sit down with the Lord today, jot down what you feel He is speaking to your heart.

_____

_____

_____

_____

_____

_____

_____

_____

_____

_____

_____

_____

38

We Build A Church

"Unless The Lord builds the house they labor in vain."
Psalm 127:1

One day while volunteering in the children's nursery, I struggled to understand what little Joseph was trying to say. After guessing at this and that, I finally got it! "We build a church?"

"Yes!" he said as he made a beeline straight to the colorful cardboard building blocks.

Brick by brick, he worked along. Once it was finished, he squeezed his little body inside. When I realized how cramped he was, I tried to sneak the bricks outward just a tad. No way. The second my hand touched the first brick, he looked at me as if to say," What do you think you're doing?"

Within seconds, *he* looked around and noticed he couldn't move an inch. With such a cute little smirk he tilted his head my way then began pushing the bricks outward on his own.

Isn't that just the way we are with God? We ask for His guidance and direction when we face an important decision. The Holy Spirit tries to nudge us along. But we go on trying to build our own church until God confronts us and allows us to see that we are trying to do it our own way.

Then, the same as little Joseph turned to me when he found he couldn't move, we humbly turn back to God and say, "All right Lord, I'm in a pinch, now *what* is it You were trying to show me?"

In all reality my beloved, the first step that we need to take is truly the most important—We need to believe the words of the Psalmist, *Unless the Lord builds the house they labor in vain.* Of course this does not mean to literally build a house, but in whatever God has called us to do, maybe write, maybe speak, maybe even caring for the elderly, whatever it is, we want Him to open the doors, and to guide us along.

So as this day begins, look at your life. See what He has called and destined you to be. Then, sit with Him and trust that His Spirit will be the greatest contractor to lead you, and to guide you in everything that comes your way.

Prayer: Dear Lord, help me to listen to You and to heed to the promptings of Your Holy Spirit. Forgive me for the times that I have tried to proceed and to go forward on my own.

As you sit down with the Lord today, jot down what you feel He is speaking to your heart.

_____

_____

_____

_____

_____

_____

_____

_____

_____

_____

_____

_____

39

Word Choices

"Peace I leave with you; my peace I give you. I do not give to you as the world gives. Do not let your hearts be troubled and do not be afraid."
John 14:27

"Grandma, we've got a problem!"

This is a favorite phrase of my grandson, Cesare. Whenever he says it, I always respond the same; "No, Cesare, we do not have a problem, we have an opportunity to watch God find a solution for us."

You see, we will always have problems that arise. That's a given. But it is our choice how to handle them. We can either allow fear to well up on the inside of us and begin to drive us crazy, or we can take it to the Lord and say, "What are *we* going to do about this?"

The sooner we learn to turn it over to God, the sooner we will be able to experience peace in our life. I firmly believe if I can teach this to my grandson at nine years old, he will definitely have a more peaceful life than I did.

And my beloved it is the same for you. The more you stay in the Bible and learn the promises that God has for you— especially in the Gospels of Matthew, Mark, Luke, and John where Jesus speaks directly to us—you will have an easier time of making the choice to take your problem to him as soon as you become aware of it.

Remember, Jesus said that He comes to give us peace for a reason. He knew that the world would be full of chaos. He knew that we would be unable to handle it on our own. And He also knew that every single day we would have obstacles that would arise out of the uncertainty before us. That is why He says, "I will give you peace but not as the world gives."

You see, the world's peace is superficial. It is never long-lasing. Granted, it may suppress our problems for the moment and bring us what we need for now, but Jesus's peace is everlasting. It is for now in this life that we are living and by His grace, it will stream all the way into eternity.

So, today the choice is yours. What will you do the next time a problem arises? Will you respond like Cesare, "We have a problem," or will you choose to make a conscious choice to ask, "Lord, what are we going to do about this today?"

Prayer for the day: Dear Jesus, I most certainly want and need Your peace. Help me to remember to choose to call upon You to help defeat every problem that I will face today. I thank You that I am not alone in any problem that may come along.

As you sit down with the Lord today, jot down what you feel He is speaking to your heart.

_____

_____

_____

_____

_____

_____

_____

_____

_____

_____

_____

_____

40

You Are Near

"Surely he will save you from the fowler's snare
and from the deadly pestilence. He will cover you with his
feathers,
and under his wings you will find refuge;
His faithfulness will be your shield and rampart."
Psalm 91:3-4

Grandchildren are truly a blessing from the Lord.

Today we took our grandchildren to see a cute movie about pets. We laughed and cried together. When a scary scene appeared on the screen, my granddaughter hopped over her brother and snuggled up on my lap. Just when a scary part appeared on the screen, she buried her head in my shoulder to seek comfort.

I suddenly thought of the verse, *"And under His wings, you will take refuge."*

Just like my granddaughter needed shelter to hide during that scene of the movie, we, too, are the same. We too

157

experience things in our lives that make us fearful. Health issues, financial dilemmas, work pressures and the list goes on. But just like my little granddaughter, Giuliana, she knew she could hop over and find comfort in Grandma's arms. She could hide from the bit of evil she saw and cover her little eyes until the scary stuff was over.

We are so blessed that we have an Abba Father that we can run to when things of this world bring us fear. And fear is not a respecter of persons. Fear can attack us at any age. It can attack us not only at any age, but at different seasons of our lives.

Beloved, God is just waiting with open arms, as I was with little Giuliana, for us to come to Him. Take some time today and read the entire Psalm 91. It will not only bring you comfort for today, but in the days to come. It is one of the Psalms in the Bible that will have a lasting effect on your life.

Know that no matter what comes your way, God is our refuge. He is our fortress and if we dwell in His shadow, then He will always be there to protect us. And beloved, as you read down to verse eleven, this one is a keeper, *He will command his angels concerning you to guard you in all your ways*; What a precious promise from our Abba Father!

Not only will he protect you as I protected Giuliana, but he will command His angels to guard you. Let's be real. Where on earth can we find that protection? We know it's only from a loving and faithful God. So today, no matter what scary scene of life is playing before you, turn to your Heavenly Father and bury your burdens beneath the shadow of His mighty wings.

Prayer for the day: Dear Father, You know all the scary stuff that sometimes comes before me. You know that I try so hard to face it on my own. But how good it is to know that when it sometimes gets too much, I can simply run to You. Thank You for always being there, no matter the time of day, that I can find refuge in Your precious and loving arms.

As you sit down with the Lord today, jot down what you feel He is speaking to your heart.

_____

_____

_____

_____

_____

_____

_____

_____

_____

_____

_____

ABOUT THE AUTHOR

Del has a desire to bring the message of God's love to everyone she comes in contact with. In December of 2000 she self-published her first book titled *Journey With The Lord*. Continuing to pursue her calling, she began attending writing conferences to learn the craft. Her heart in writing steers between Daily Devotionals and Children.

Since then she has been published in *The Upper Room*, *Women of The Harvest and The War Cry*. She has stories published in *Nudges From God* and *God's Handprint, The Healing Touch* and *Christmas Miracles*.

She has been involved in MOPS (Mothers of Preschoolers) as a mentor and speaker, and has worked with children through Vacation Bible School programs. As a member of the leadership team for Community Bible Study in Vero Beach, she thoroughly enjoyed working in the children's ministry.

Presently she is the President of her local Aglow Lighthouse in Vero Beach; www.verobeachaglow.com

After retiring from their former business, Del and her husband are enjoying their new life as snowbirds between Florida and Michigan where they enjoy spending time with their children, family, and five precious grandchildren.